THE BIG THICK JOE PASQUALE BOOK

THE BIG THICK JOE PASQUALE BOOK

ALAN WIGHTMAN & JOE PASQUALE

CHAMELEON

First published in Great Britain in 1996 by
Chameleon Books
106 Great Russell Street
London WC1B 3LJ

CIP data for this title is available from the British Library

ISBN 0 233 99049 6

Printed in Great Britain by Bath Press Colourbooks, Glasgow

JOE PASQUALE LIVE AND SQUEAKY is available on video.
Catalogue number VC6554. It is also available on audio cassette from MCI.
Catalogue number GAGSDMC051

READY STEADY GO!

IT'S MY KIND OF DAY

My alarm clock usually goes off around **6.00 a.m.** but I never hear it because I lent it to a mate of mine two years ago. If I've been working in a nightclub or theatre and climb into bed around **3. 00 a.m.**, my wife is incredibly understanding and tiptoes out of bed to practice on her tuba in the wardrobe. Try as she might to keep the noise down, **I do** sometimes hear the odd note seeping from under the wardrobe door. On those very rare occasions, I just shrug my shoulders, give a little grin and go down to the kitchen. I then fill a four-pint jug with cold porridge, go back upstairs and pour it down her tuba.

The number of times we've collapsed with laughter at that jape!

Less than once, from memory.

On a normal day, the dogs bound into the bedroom around 7.00 a.m. and tear around the bed like a couple of thoroughbred racehorses. Some days the thoroughbred racehorses bound into the bedroom and tear around the bed like a couple of dogs. Each day is so different ...

Around 7.30 a.m. the children are demanding their breakfasts, so my wife and I have a daily roster worked out, otherwise we'd never be able to cope with their huge appetites! On Sundays, Tuesdays, Thursdays and Fridays, I get the chance to say to them 'Look, you're 18 and 20! Get your own flippin' breakfasts' and my wife gets to say it the rest of the week. I make sure the kids are both gone by 8.30 a.m. and I know they'll be out of the house until tea-time. They don't like sitting on the front doorstep for ten hours, but to be fair, I don't like them hanging around inside the house all day. Well, it's not healthy.

My wife drives to the office around 8.45 a.m. I've never understood why since it's right next to the downstairs' loo.

By the time I've put some washing in the machine, dried the dishes, ironed a few shirts, gone around with the vacuum cleaner and taken the dogs for a walk, it's almost time for coffee, 8.50 a.m.

As I look out of the kitchen window, I see our postman, whose name isn't Pat, incidentally, wheeling his bike up the drive. He always gives me a cheery wave and I always ignore him, otherwise he'll expect a Christmas bonus and I don't believe in tipping tradesmen.

I spend at least an hour ploughing through my mail. Then I put the plough back in the shed and clean the mess up. A lot of my mail is made up of invitations to showbiz parties and first nights and Royal Gala premieres, but I throw them away. I just wouldn't feel right turning up on the night holding a gold invitation in my hand. I hate all that shallow, 'You look mah-velous darling' showbiz insincerity. Besides, Stewart Granger used to live in my house and they're all addressed to him.

Every morning, from 10.00 a.m. until 11.00 a.m., I answer my fan mail. I only get one letter a day, but I'm a very slow writer. Then it's time for my ten-mile run through some of the wildest countryside in Lewisham. By the time I've run five miles, the sweat's dripping off me, my legs are aching and I can hardly breathe, so I let go of the back of the bus and then I usually feel a lot better.

On the way back home I stop off at a little greasy-spoon café I've been going to for years. The proprietor takes care of me and makes sure I have exactly the same greasy spoon every day.

I spend most afternoons at the gym. I think we have a duty to look after our bodies, because no one else is going to look after them for us, so I generally ease myself on to an empty bench and get down to a couple of hours of serious kip.

If I'm not working during the evening, I might cook us a light dinner - something Italian and romantic. A deliciously wicked spaghetti carbonara with lightly browned garlic bread and a crisp green salad, or maybe a cheese and chutney doorstep with a packet of salt and vinegar crisps on the side, washed down with a pint of milk straight out of the bottle.

I might switch on the TV, but only if there's a wildlife documentary on, because that's the only type of show that people who write about 'their kind of day' ever admit they watch. At the last count, this must mean that 44 million people only watch wildlife documentaries, and a mere nine people watch my shows, which isn't very good news, is it? For a start, I've got 11,796 relatives who obviously don't give a toss about my career.

I might read a book in bed - something by one of the great novelists, or Jeffrey Archer. Then I switch out the light, at 10.30 p.m. sharp. This really gets up my wife's nose, 'cos she likes to read until 10.45 p.m. I wonder if that's got anything to do with her early morning tuba lessons?

FEELING LETHARGIC?

WANT TO GET FIT, BUT THE GYM FEES ARE TOO EXPENSIVE? DON'T WORRY!!

There's a **CHEAPER** way to change the shape of your body! *Send for my video -*

'KEEP FIT THE JOE PASQUALE WAY'

Yes, for only £14.99 you can shape up in the comfort of your own home, depending on how comfortable your own home is. 'KEEP FIT THE JOE PASQUALE WAY' is the easy way to tone up those muscles. Here's the major technological breakthrough that other keep-fit videos can't offer you!

MY 'KEEP FIT THE JOE PASQUALE WAY' VIDEO CAN FIRM YOUR FLAB AND GET YOU FIGHTING FIT EVEN IF YOU DON'T HAVE A VIDEO RECORDER!!

When the tape arrives, place it in your right hand and **raise your arm 20 times**, then place it in your left hand and **raise THAT arm 20 times**. Repeat until you feel the benefit, or you tear your shoulder muscles and require major surgery.

GET TWICE AS FIT!! WHY NOT SEND FOR TWO KEEP FIT VIDEOS - ONE FOR EACH ARM!

'KEEP FIT THE JOE PASQUALE WAY' *comes with a 14 day guarantee which runs out the day before you receive it.*

We accept all major credit cards - and one or two dodgy ones.

BUY FOUR AND MAKE ME RICHER!

PASQ
ON
PETS

I talk to the animals and they *totally ignore me*

UALE

Hello animal lovers, which includes me. So, hello me! Yes,

I've always been fond of animals and they seem to like me too. For example, I've never once been stung by a cow. How many of us can say that these days?

When I was a little lad, we always had pets.

A pet can bring love and joy into your home. Mostly they bring fleas and dead mice. These days fleas are very easy to treat. Take them to the pictures and buy them a bag of chips on the way home and they'll be delighted.

One of the first pets I can remember having was a goat. My dad bought him to keep the grass short and he was very good at it. But in all the years we had him, he never **once** cleaned the lawn mower after he'd finished using it.

I had two fluffy white bunny rabbits - Mr Flopsy and Mr Topsy. Although they looked identical, they were entirely different. Mr Flopsy tasted delicious, while Mr Topsy was a bit chewy.

Cats are funny animals, aren't they? But they hardly ever use any topical material. Have you noticed that?

If you really care for your cat, get him neutered by a vet. If you're not that keen on it, I know a postman who'll do it for a tenner.

For my tenth birthday, my parents promised me something really noisy that had a ladder and a bell. I thought I was going to have a fire engine, but they got me a budgie.

If ever I want to stay up all night and party, I nibble on some cuttlefish. Well it works for budgies. Unless you throw a cloth over their cage they'd sing for 24 hours a day.

Hamsters are cute, furry animals who don't ask much out of life - mainly because they can't talk.

The big drawback with hamsters is that they have a very short life span. The hamster motto being:

'Live fast, die young, leave plenty of clean straw in your cage.'

Tortoises have to be the most useless pets of all. You buy them, then you have to put them away in a shoe box for six months! Where's the value for money in that? You wouldn't buy a car off someone who told you that you had to leave it in the garage all through the winter, would you?

I had a tortoise when I was nine, but he didn't last very long. It was my mum's fault - she was so used to ironing **everything** before she put it in the airing cupboard.

Parrots can live to a great age, so make sure you teach yours plenty of words. Otherwise, by the time he gets to 80, he'll have run out of things to talk about.

We had a parrot, and instead of keeping it in a cage, we let him have the run of the house. One day when we were out, he sold it to an old couple from Bognor.

Minah birds have the uncanny knack of being

able to mimic the human voice. Unfortunately, the only two expressions they can master are:

'Good morning!'
and **'Lovely day!'** -
the same limited vocabulary as my next door neighbour.

Terrapins are basically tortoises that swim. Any terrapin that can't swim is called 'a drowning tortoise'.

Tarantula spiders can be useful when you've invited friends over and towards the end of the evening the conversation starts to flag. Believe me, you've only got to say

'My tarantula's escaped!'

and things will liven up almost immediately.

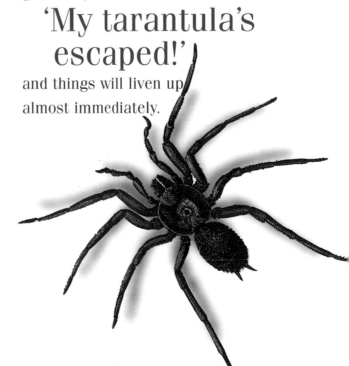

Tropical fish can be very pretty to look at, but when it comes to making small talk they're rubbish. I'm just telling you in case you see one at a party and think it might be worth chatting to.

I bought some tropical fish once, but I didn't have to buy a tank to put them in. I already had a great big one at home, and it was already full of water, but it can be a bit of a nuisance, having to go up to the loft every time they need feeding.

It's not true what they say about dogs. You can teach an old dog new tricks. But they're not very good at close-up magic because you can always tell which card they want you to pick. It's the one covered in dribble.

Dalmatians are beautiful animals, though having that spotted coat does bring one big disadvantage. A dalmatian could never get away with wearing a

striped tie.

A Dachshund is a dog that has a long body and little legs. If you come home from the pet shop with something that has a little body and long legs, you've bought a frog.

An Alsatian is a top deterrent to burglars, especially if you hang a flashing light round its neck, paint it a bright shiny red and place it on the front of your house.

St. Bernards wander aimlessly around the Swiss Alps carrying large supplies of strong alcohol. A bit like British tourists, really.

A Chihuahua is one of the world's tiniest dogs. In fact it's so tiny, chihuahua is a Mexican word meaning

'Oi! I'm down here!'

Scotty dogs are good company, but do tend to say the same things day after day. Like:

'She cannae hold for much longer Captain!'

or

'My dilithium crystals are about to explode any minute Mr Spock!'

Boxer dogs are very popular, but do bear in mind that they won't fight other dogs unless there's a million pound purse at stake. Also, after a short career, they often turn nasty and become sports commentators.

Collies are rather lovely and are on special offer this week at my local greengrocers.

White mice look really cute with their little pink noses and tails and they always go down well as a birthday gift. I get my cat one every year.

WELL, THAT'S THE PASQUALE GUIDE TO PETS.

If you haven't got a pet and you're thinking of buying one, always remember to treat it with kindness and respect. In many ways, animals are like people. For example, they can't get tickets for 'Phantom Of The Opera' or find a parking space on Saturday mornings.

Treat your pets well and you'll be friends for life. Treat them badly and they'll take off to Marbella with your wife and run up a credit card bill you'd never be able to pay off, not even if you won the Lottery every week for a year.

So, next time you're at the fairground and you think it might be fun to win a goldfish, just pause for a minute before you throw those ping-pong balls at the glass bowls and think about the trouble you could be making for yourself!

History's Forgotten Heroes Remembered

Nick Turpin

I'm fascinated by history and I've hundreds of books on the subject at home. The more history books I read, the more I'm convinced of one thing. They're going to go potty down the library if I don't start taking them back.

When we were taught history at school, it was all about dates. Dates of battles, dates of Kings' birthdays, dates of Queens' deaths. Well, I don't mind stating right here that I don't give a fig for dates!

To me, history is all about people. The people who made the world what it is. Explorers, warriors, sailors, soldiers, adventurers ... and the person who we should all be grateful to - the man who invented the underarm deodorant. It's all very well being proud of Lord Nelson or the Duke Of Wellington, but it's not **them** *I'm grateful to when I'm crammed on to a crowded Tube train in the middle of a July heatwave and a seven-foot back-packer's got his armpit under my nose!*

I want to tell you about the great characters in history you've never heard about. *There are all sorts of reasons why they're unknown. Mainly it's because when their*

moment of glory came, there was nobody around to write it all down. This was particularly sad in the case of the man who invented the exercise book. It would be another ten years before someone else invented the pencil.

You certainly wouldn't have heard of **Nick Turpin**. Nick was the young cousin of the famous highwayman Dick Turpin, and also, quite interestingly, a distant relative of a very funny comedian of the silent film era whose career was sadly overshadowed by the likes of *Chaplin*, *Keaton* and *Harold Lloyd*: the cross-eyed clown *Ben Turpin* (1874-1940).

Nick Turpin wasn't supposed to follow in his cousin's footsteps. By trade he was a newsagent, which wasn't really much of a trade in those days as there was only one daily paper. It had only one page and it used to be pinned up outside the Town Hall so that everyone had access to it.

Nick was resigned to the fact he'd never make a fortune as a newsagent. Now he knew that Dick Turpin was a highwayman by profession, but he wasn't sure what a highwayman actually did for a living. So one day, when Dick went out to rob the London to Bath stagecoach,

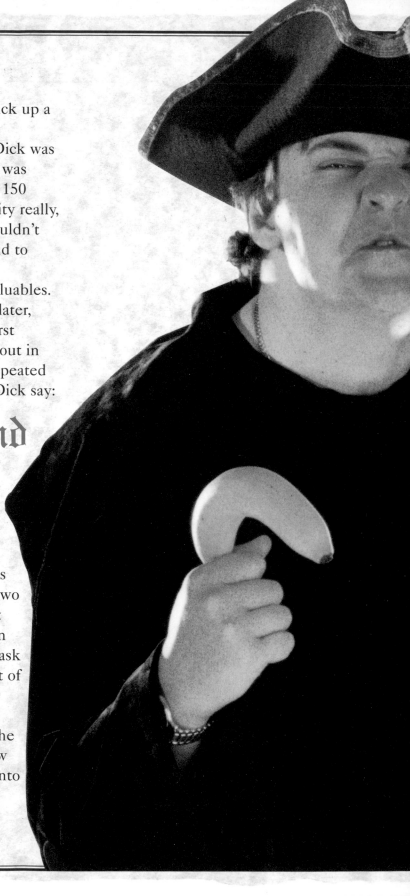

he followed him, hoping to pick up a few tips.

At the precise moment Dick was robbing the stagecoach, Nick was watching from behind a bush 150 yards away. It was a bit of a pity really, 'cos being that far away he couldn't really hear what Dick had said to make the driver stop and the passengers hand over their valuables.

As a result, a few weeks later, when Nick went out on his first highway robbery, he stepped out in front of the stagecoach and repeated what he thought he'd heard Dick say:

'I can't stand raw liver!'

You may possibly have noticed that this made no sense whatsoever. When you also consider that the weapons Nick held in his hands were two large bananas (in the dimly lit kitchen he thought he'd taken two bread-knives), and the mask he wore around the lower part of his face was something he'd improvised using a gingham tablecloth with a lacy frill at the bottom, you'll understand how the entire episode dissolved into a complete farce.

Sensing he had possibly used the wrong expression,

Nick tried out different variations on the stagecoach driver.

'I CAN stand raw liver!'

'Stand up and slither!'

'Ask the band to play 'Cry Me a River.'

'Hand me a grand wrapped in liver!'

But he still couldn't get the wording right.

After patiently putting up with this for the best part of twenty minutes, the stagecoach driver just shook his head and tutted, snapped the reins and drove away, while the half-dozen bemused passengers, watching this nervous little man angrily brandishing two bananas recede into the distance, put all their valuables back in their pockets and handbags.

As Nick dejectedly made his way home, he decided that he might **just** have got away with it if he'd committed the crime while on horseback instead of sitting astride his Uncle Harold's prize sow.

After that one lapse Nick kept to the straight and narrow. He got a job on a canal barge.

Kevin

There was a little seal called Kevin,
Who could balance big balls on his nose,
So he tried to join several circuses,
But they all said 'Sorry, we've got one
of those!'
So he tried to break into cabaret,
After polishing up his class act,
But he failed at every audition,
I'm not making this up, it's a fact!
So eventually, sad and disheartened,
He knocked on the gates of a zoo,
And asked if they'd consider taking
him in,
They said 'Hmmm, can you play drums
and kazoo?'
He said 'No, but I am a quick learner'
They said 'That's no good, the dance starts
in an hour',
But they let him come in and gave him a room
It had colour TV and a shower.

He became the zoo's mega attraction,
People stared at him while they
ate lunch,
And when they discussed all the
beasts on display,
They said 'Kevin's the best of
the bunch!'
But Kevin got bored just
balancing balls,
So he took an 'A' level in
Greek,
Then he went up to Oxford
- and Cambridge as well,
And got his degree in a
week!
This phenomenal seal was
offered a job
By a firm making satellite dishes,
Now he's the only director on the board
Who gets paid in big barrels of fishes!

NINETEEN FASCINATING FACTS ABOUT ME

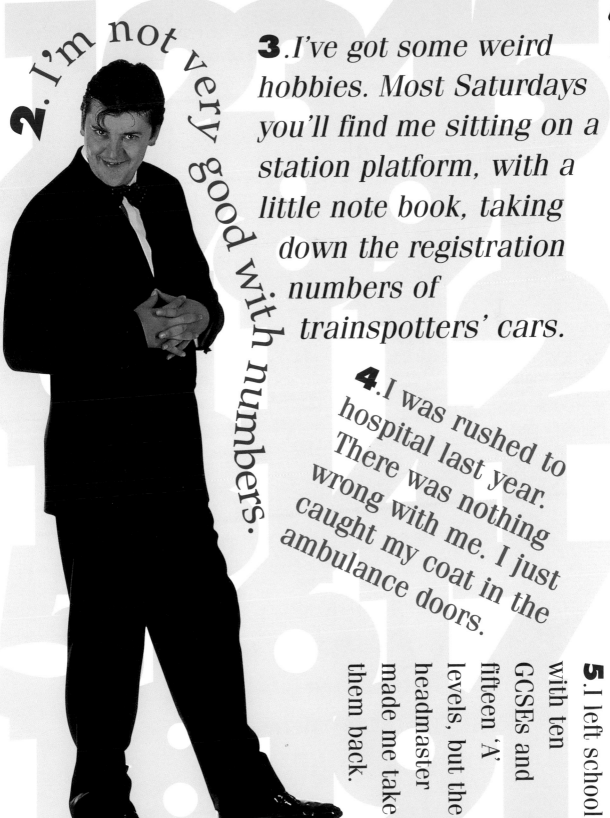

2. I'm not very good with numbers.

3. *I've got some weird hobbies. Most Saturdays you'll find me sitting on a station platform, with a little note book, taking down the registration numbers of trainspotters' cars.*

4. I was rushed to hospital last year. There was nothing wrong with me. I just caught my coat in the ambulance doors.

5. I left school with ten GCSEs and fifteen 'A' levels, but the headmaster made me take them back.

6.I'm very superstitious. Some people carry a rabbit's foot around with them for luck, but I'm four times luckier than them. I carry a RABBIT around with me!

7.When I was ten, I decided I'd like to solve crimes when I grew up. I almost achieved my ambition. I've helped the police with their enquiries several times.

8.I once went to the doctors with chronic insomnia and he told me to go home and sleep it off!

9.When I was fifteen, I went to a fortune teller in Blackpool who told me that one day I would hit the heights. Just after I left her tent, I walked straight into the side of Blackpool Tower and needed twenty-seven stitches.

10.*People often ask me what sign I was born under and my usual reply is 'How did you get in my bathroom, anyway?' In fact, I was born under a very special sign. It said MATERNITY WARD in big red letters on a white background.*

11.When I was growing up, I had a very happy home. The three-piece suite was always splitting its sides giggling. In fact there were times when my house was so full of laughter, my family had to move out to my mum's sister's house in Broadstairs until there was enough space for us to move back in.

12.I was a boy soprano and thought I could have made a career out of it, but when I got to 13, the penny finally dropped.

13. *My dad was a policeman, but he never rose above the rank of Constable. This might have had something to do with the fact that the first time he was asked to go under cover, he went out and bought a duvet. He spent 30 years in uniform, despite my mum's many requests that he should take it off once in a while so that she could wash it.*

14. I carry a donor card everywhere, on which is written 'IN THE EVENT OF AN ACCIDENT, GIVE THIS MAN A KEBAB.'

16. While on holiday in Africa, I was attacked by a rogue elephant. The hotel manager had no idea how it got into the lift.

15. I'm already in training for next year's London Marathon. I'm now at the stage where I can hand out 500 cups of water in an hour without getting a stitch.

17. As one of the film industry's top stuntmen, I've doubled for many top stars when a sequence was too dangerous for them. Remember that jump off the top of the dam that Pierce Brosnan made at the beginning of 'Goldeneye'? That wasn't Pierce, that was me.

Harrison Ford's last minute leap out of the way of that speeding train in 'The Fugitive'? Look carefully next time you see that film. It's not Harrison, it's me! And that famous Buster Keaton moment when the front of the house started to collapse, but he escaped injury by inches because he was standing where the open window would land? OK, that was Buster Keaton. Good, wasn't it?

18. Now do you believe I'm not very good with numbers?

HEY MUS

WOULD YOU LIKE TO SEE THE ROLLING STONES IN BELGIUM? OR PHIL COLLINS AND GENESIS IN PARIS?

Then send your **£49.99** to

'Rockin' Joe Promotions' No. 1 (after six weeks at No. 3) Thatwass Close, Towcester, Crumbs.

And we'll send you a pair of

HIGH-POWERED BINOCULARS.

(with free 'string-look' string)

Just stand on any cliff top along the south coast, look through your binoculars and you'll see your fave bands 'live' in Europe without having to go to all the expense of coach and ferry travel and trying to purchase those oh-so-hard-to-come-by concert tickets

'ROCKIN' JOE PROMOTIONS'

WE PUT YOU IN THE FRONT ROW!!

Sadly, although you should be able to see the band of your choice, you won't be able to hear them

No. Not even **'ROCKIN' JOE'** can let you hear a concert that's happening over 100 miles away!

Can he?
Oh yes he can!!

If you also send him an extra **£49.99** for one of his sensational **'ROCKIN' JOE'** personal sound boosters*, with an on AND off switch and a little pink plastic thing that fits snugly into your ear, you won't miss a note of that **Channel-hoppin', ever-boppin' Rooooccccckkkk and rooolllllll!!**

GIVE ME A BREAK

What's the most exciting word in the English language? It's got seven letters and starts with an 'H'. I know nine out of ten of you will shout out **'Hypogene!'**, the word we all tend to over use, the one that describes rocks that are formed beneath the earth's surface. My milkman brought the word up just today. But at 4.39 a.m. I was fast asleep in bed, so I missed his merry banter. But no, hypogene is **not** the most exciting word in the English language. The most exciting word is

Holiday!

Yes, it **is** an exciting word, isn't it? I've only just written it down and I've already started packing, cancelled the papers and blown a big kiss at the wall-length picture of Judith Chalmers that greets visitors in my hall.

We all need holidays in these dog-eat-dog times, don't we? Not that I've ever seen one dog tucking in to another.

Do you know what a fortnight's holiday represents? It's two weeks out of the 52, when we can do whatever we please. Two weeks a year when we're not just a number on a pay slip or an income tax form.

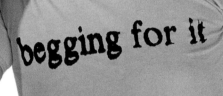

Two weeks a year when we can be ourselves, and not just one of the crowd; individuals with our own specific personal thoughts and dreams.

So, being the strong-minded, rugged, non-conforming types,

how do we choose to spend our hard-earned break? We sit on a plane with 350 others who are all flying to the same bit of the Costa. We all stay at the same resort in exactly the same hotel and all our rooms are on the same floor. And on the first morning we are all to be found huddled around a swimming pool that holds less water than a flannel.

Something that's very popular these days is the last-minute holiday. To be honest, I've never understood the concept of a last-minute holiday. Why do people let it sneak up on them like that? I always know exactly when I'm going on holiday, because I write it down on the calendar, months before, so that I won't forget. Why don't they?

When it came to holidays, my dad was always a stickler for tradition. I can't ever remember him being a stickler for anything else, but he was a pickler for an onion factory once. He took the same two weeks off work every year - always the first week in July and the last week in August.

His holiday arrangements made our going away for a complete fortnight a bit awkward. In fact, it made going away for a fortnight totally out of the question, so we always used to have a week's holiday 'here' and another week's holiday 'there'. Out of the two, I preferred to have a holiday 'there', because I already lived 'here'.

The most disappointing year for me, as far as holidays were concerned, was when I was six. Like a lot of kids, I had an imaginary friend I used to play with. That July, mum and dad took him on holiday and left me with my nan.

We never had a holiday abroad. That was because my mum was scared of flying and my dad had an irrational fear of hand-luggage.

We never went to the seaside, because my mum was allergic to sand and my dad had an irrational fear of 'I Speak Your Weight' machines and whelks.

We didn't even go on holiday to the country because anything

green brought my mum out in a purple rash from head to toe. Well, not just ONE toe; all eight of them. I daren't give you a complete explanation of why she was minus two. Let's just say there was an 'incident' involving open-toed sandals and the sharp, rotating steel blades of a high-powered lawnmower!

I think my dad would have liked to have spent a holiday in the country, but my mum wouldn't tell him where it was.

The best holiday I ever had was when I was 20 and I set off to back-pack around Europe. I arrived at Southampton docks knowing that if I was heading for foreign shores, I'd need a strong, sturdy ship. I made it my business to seek out the finest craft lashed to the quayside. There she was, gleaming in the heat of the midday sun. A barnacle encrusted, weather-beaten old sloop. But she had a lovely smile. I asked her if she knew where I could find a passage to the Continent and she said, *'I'm not sure about any passage, but there's this tunnel thing that leads to France that they've built down Folkestone way, so they tell me.'*

I thanked her for her help and dropped a pound into her tin cup. She discovered it moments after I left her, nearly choking on it as she swigged her tea. I wandered along the quayside looking for a likely craft to take me away from the land of my birth.

'Ahoy there!'

bellowed a one-eyed old sea dog sitting on a salt-stained poop deck. I'd never heard a dog talk before, let alone one with an eye missing. Then I looked again and saw it wasn't the dog that had spoken. It was his master, the grizzled Captain of the vessel named *The Saucy Innuendo*, who stood behind him. He stopped grizzling and cheered up a bit. *'Will ye be looking for a passage to the Continent, me fine laddo?'* he asked, as he whittled. Try as I might, I didn't recognise the tune he was whittling.

'Aye, Aye Captain!' I replied, instantly lapsing into authentic sea dog talk. All those hours I'd spent travelling to and fro on the Woolwich Ferry were paying off.

'Are ye now?' said the weather-beaten old man, scratching his white beard with the metal hook that replaced his right hand. *'Well, there b'aint' be no passage round these parts. But there's this tunnel thing that leads to France they've built down Folkestone way, so they tell me!'*

I didn't want the chance to pass me by. I had to ask him now. It was getting late and he might be sailing on the evening tide. 'Is there any chance of some work aboard your ship, Captain?'

He looked me up and down with a rheumy eye. It was so rheumy, a family of four from Truro had moved in and were planning to extend the kitchen and put a study in the loft. *'So, you'd like to try out your sea legs, would you me bucko?'* he guffawed.

'That I would, Cap'n,' I chortled.

'Well, climb aboard and let's take a look at ye,' he chuckled.

'Permission to come aboard?' I giggled.

'Granted,' he tittered.

I reflected that if nothing else, a life on the high seas seemed to require a highly developed sense of humour.

I walked up the gangplank, avoiding the gang, and as I planted my two feet firmly on the deck, I realised that having a dog on board had its disadvantages. I also realised why it was called the poop deck.

I ducked and the shot missed me. The Captain shook my hand, but there was no need. It was already shaking. He said he'd take me on for a trial period without wages, though I offered him fifty quid a week. He asked me if I knew the difference between a mainbrace and a fo'c'sle and when I hung my head in shame and told him I didn't have a clue, he was very disappointed. It turned out he didn't have a clue either and was hoping I could tell him.

'So where are we bound on tonight's tide?' I asked him, as he tied a thick sailor's knot in Jonah's tail.

'We bain't be sailing anywhere tonight, me laddo, me bucko, me son o'the sea,' he replied.

'We only sets out during daylight hours. The customers prefers it that way.'

'Customers?' I parried.

'Yes, customers,' he parried back, almost slicing my ear off with his sharp-bladed scimitar. He was an expert at fencing, having once erected thirty-three six-foot panels in less than a day. A man like that could lead an entire armada to victory!

'I make my living taking city folks out into the Channel for a day's fishing. I gets a hundred

quid in me hand ... the good one ... and they gets to think they're Captain Ahab for a couple of hours.'

'Well, just how far out to sea do you go in this ship?' I asked tentatively.

'Oh, about half a mile,' he replied.

unpleasant habit to behold. He had obviously never owned a hankie in his life.

'Before I go, I have two questions to ask,' I said, gathering up my belongings.

'I know what the first question is,' he nodded sagely, chewing a handful of herbs. He quickly held his steel hook up to the light, a little too quickly actually as it tore

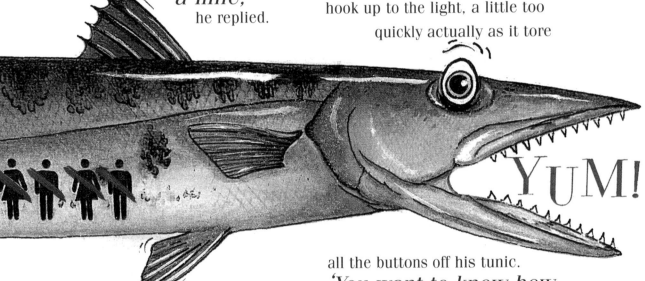

YUM!

'I'm sorry,' I sighed. 'You're not going far enough for me. I can't limit my horizons. The open sea is calling me.'

'I can just imagine WHAT it's calling you too,' he snorted. It was a most

all the buttons off his tunic.

'You want to know how I lost my hand, don't you?' he asked.

'Did a barracuda do that to you?' I asked, as I made myself comfortable on a load of sacking. I'd read in the papers that they were having loads of sackings in the fishing industry.

'No, a nice doctor in Southampton Hospital fitted it on for me,' he said, tapping it gently with his good hand. 'And I'm proud to say I didn't have it done private. No,

this is an NHS fisherman's hook,' he said, as it fell to the deck with a clang. He bent down to pick it up, but couldn't quite reach. I was going to offer to give him a hand, but so far I've tried to avoid too many obvious jokes.

Eventually he picked

it up, having twice tried to do so with the wrist the hook had dropped from. He may have been an expert on fish, but basically he was one prawn short of a cocktail.

'Twas a great white shark what done it,' he said, replacing the hook. 'I should have seen it coming. But after all these years sailing the world, I let my guard down just for a second and he had me!'

'Where did it happen? Off the warm waters of the Azores? In a blue lagoon off Pago Pago? Or were you adrift in the middle of the Pacific as a pitiless, merciless sun beat down on you?' I desperately needed to know.

He shook his head. As he did so, small clouds of long forgotten talcum powder fell from his head and a spider did a spectacular somersault from his ear-ring.

'I was just reaching in the water to retrieve my watch, which had fallen in, and there he was. Eighteen feet of killing machine, looking up at me with that cold eye of his. He clamped his teeth down on my hand and took it away for his tea.'

He opened his mouth wide to laugh and I saw he didn't have a tooth in his head - they were all in his mouth.

'Yes, but in what lonely part of the world did this happen?' I asked.

'Oh, down at the Sea Life Centre. It was my first

time in one of those places and I shan't be going back there in a hurry! What's your other question?'

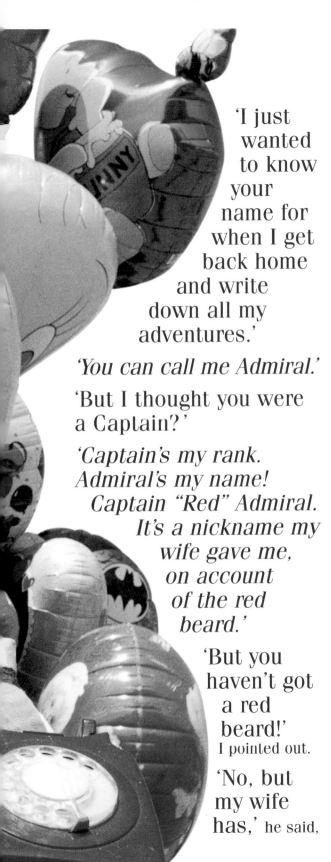

'I just wanted to know your name for when I get back home and write down all my adventures.'

'You can call me Admiral.'

'But I thought you were a Captain?'

'Captain's my rank. Admiral's my name! Captain "Red" Admiral. It's a nickname my wife gave me, on account of the red beard.'

'But you haven't got a red beard!' I pointed out.

'No, but my wife has,' he said,

and he began to whittle again. I suddenly recognised the tune. It was 'I've Never Been to Me', a number one hit for Charlene in the June of 1982. How strange that he should know that particular melody. He looked to me more like a 'Pump Up the Volume' type of guy. You never can tell. Written and recorded by Chuck Berry.

I thanked him for offering me the job and he said that if I changed my mind he'd be sailing with half a dozen city folks at 6.30 a.m. the next day. But I planned to be many miles away by then.

So I phoned my dad and asked him if he'd pick me up at the station at about midnight.

That was the year I set out to back-pack around Europe, but didn't quite make it. Instead, I ended up working as a geologist's assistant all summer. Well how else did you think a complete bonehead like me would have heard of a clever word like

'hypogene'?

History's Forgotten Heroes Remembered

Wally Raleigh

Wally was Sir Walter Raleigh's great-uncle. He was a much greater sailor and explorer than his famous nephew, but being a very shy man he didn't like to boast about the fact that he'd made half a dozen voyages to America when Sir Walter was still playing with model boats in his bath. In fact, the only way he could prove to his wife that he wasn't two-timing her every time he disappeared for a year or so, was to bring things back from America that people in Britain were unfamiliar with at the time. Like clean underwear, nostril-hair tweezers and soap.

By the time he'd made his third and fourth voyages to America, the native American Indians treated him like an old friend of the family. When they saw him coming they'd switch off all the lights in the house, draw the curtains and take the phone off the hook. Wally thought this was one of their ancient welcoming customs and would wait outside their front gate for days, thinking they were inside chanting incantations and praying to their old gods. In actual fact they were playing **Connect Four**, eating pepperoni pizzas and taking the occasional peek through the Venetian blind to see if the boring Englishman with the terrible tat he called **'Gifts from the Queen of England'**, had got the message.

Wally thought it only fair that if he took weird and wonderful things back to Britain, he should take interesting items from his homeland to show the native Americans. Polite as they were, they couldn't help but disguise their boredom when he insisted on showing them all 190 slides of his walking holiday in the Cotswolds.

The sad thing is, Wally **could** have made his mark on history and it would have been him we remember and not his nephew. You see, it was Wally Raleigh who first brought the potato from America to this country some ten years before Walter. The reason we've never read about his discovery is that on his way back home, about halfway across the Atlantic, he suddenly felt hungry. So although he enjoyed the first ever potato, he had nothing to take back home with him. He was in a bit of a jam, because he'd already written to his wife and told her he was bringing a potato home and he knew she'd have invited a few close friends and relatives round to have a look at it. She'd probably gone the whole hog and organised a **'Welcome Wally's Potato Party'.**

He was going to be in **big** trouble. He'd be faced with a roomful of people all eagerly expecting to see something exciting and world changing. Some of them were tough, uncouth characters who might turn on him! Was he to lose his life merely because of a potato?

He didn't want to end up at the bottom of the Thames, forgotten and ignored by history. Then it came to him. He'd show them all 190 slides of his walking holiday in the Cotswolds! **'Yes Wally,'** he assured himself **'That is what you're going to do!'**

And that is exactly what he did, which is why he ended up at the bottom of the Thames, forgotten and ignored by history!

CAMPING HOLIDAYS THE FACTS THE FUN THE APPALLING LACK OF PRIVACY

By the man who knows – JOE PASQUALE.

No, not by the man who knows JOE PASQUALE. By the man who KNOWS ... JOE PASQUALE.

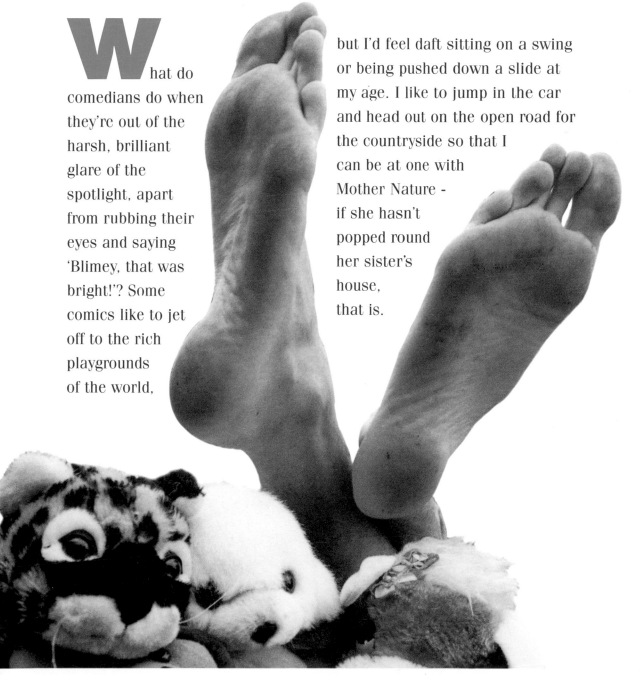

What do comedians do when they're out of the harsh, brilliant glare of the spotlight, apart from rubbing their eyes and saying 'Blimey, that was bright!'? Some comics like to jet off to the rich playgrounds of the world, but I'd feel daft sitting on a swing or being pushed down a slide at my age. I like to jump in the car and head out on the open road for the countryside so that I can be at one with Mother Nature - if she hasn't popped round her sister's house, that is.

I'm never happier than when I'm asleep under a starry sky, on a rough, makeshift bed of twigs, my tummy full of cold soup, with dozens of little furry animals around my feet. Perhaps you've stayed at the same boarding house in Taunton?

I don't mind admitting I'm a big fan of

'The Great Outdoors'.

I've got their first three albums and once met their keyboard player in a chemists in Poulton-Le-Fylde.

My first experience of the outdoor life was when I was a Cub, and I was ten at the time. In fact I was ten for an entire year. My cub pack were taken to a farm just outside. I'd like to be a little more specific about its location, but I can't remember **where** it was just outside.

The farmer had a field set aside for us and as our coach pulled up he stood outside his house, waiting for us, looking every inch the genuine rustic farmer. Corduroy trousers, corduroy waistcoat, corduroy wellies, and under his giant red hooter of a nose a little grey corduroy moustache. I can still remember his exact words.

'Lads, my name's Mr Henry Forshort-

Forshort, but you can call me Mr Forshort, for short! I bid you welcome to Sunny-Dale, Happy-View, Nasty-Smell Farm, a delightful place, as you can see. Now lads, if you're going to be living in yonder field for a week, you has to know the Country Code! 'Tis most important. Number one ... if you open a gate, you has to close him when you're finished with him. Two ... never start a fire without supervision from your Cub master. Three ... and most important of h'all ... never, ever, no matter how desperate you are, go for a widdle in a patch of stinging nettles!'

He must have really loved animals, because we heard that every night he went into the village to visit the 'black bull' and spent hours with it. It must have been quite an exhausting job, looking after such a big animal, especially as there was something wrong with it called 'rough scrumpy', which sounded really horrible.

The last camping holiday I went on was in 1986. I'd just finished a six months' summer season in a holiday camp and I was knack ... exhausted. I'd sung

'Goodnight Campers'

300 times, been thrown into the pool 400 times, and been pulled 500 times. I tell you, climbing out of that swimming pool fully clothed every day really took it out of me.

So, although it was the middle of October, I decided to have a camping holiday before the cold weather started. The first thing I had to do was buy a tent. I found a small camping shop in the middle of the High Street. It was all on its own and looked lost, so I took it to the Police Station.

They said if nobody claimed

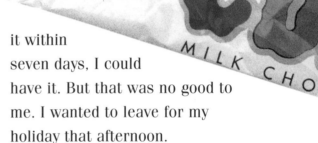

it within seven days, I could have it. But that was no good to me. I wanted to leave for my holiday that afternoon.

Then I struck lucky. Lucky was my neighbour's dog and he was always trying to bite me, so I tapped him on the nose with a rolled up copy of *Be Kind to Animals* monthly, which I'd just bought in my local newsagents. As I stood looking at all the postcards in his shop window, one in particular caught my eye, so I pulled it out of my eye and read it. It said

'Tent for sale. Suit anyone

called Joe who wants to go on holiday today. Apply within.'

But how could I apply within the tent if I didn't know where it was? I went inside and asked the newsagent.

'That postcard in your window about the tent for sale. Who's selling it?'

'I am' he said, as he lifted up a large, shapeless, green bundle from behind the counter. It was his wife, who'd slipped on a Curly Wurly wrapper in 1978 and had just come to.

'Ethel, go and get that old tent of mine.'

She shuffled into the next room, (she was an ex-member of the *Young Generation,* and shuffling was second nature to her).

To cut a long story short, I bought the tent off him, plus a whole bunch of stuff he said I'd need for an enjoyable camping holiday, including a list of comfortable hotels which he reckoned I'd find useful after three days.

He sold me a groundsheet, some ground to go with it, a sleeping bag, a bag that wasn't at all sleepy, a thick bodywarmer, his even thicker sister, one pair of stout boots and one pair of boots that had been on a diet and looked all the better for it, a mosquito net, a butterfly net, a hair net, a hurricane lamp, a rather-windy-day lamp and a what-a-lovely-gentle-breeze-that-is lamp. The newsagent wanted fifty quid for the lot, but after a bit of haggling I eventually got him to accept seventy-five. He helped me load my car and as I drove away he very courteously waved goodbye to me for the entire length of the High Street, around the ring road and along thirty miles of dual carriageway. It was only when I noticed he was still waving goodbye as I passed junction seven of the M4 that I realised his tie was caught in the nearside rear door. When I pulled in to the next services and freed the poor man, he was suitably grateful but refused my offer to give him a lift back to his shop. He said the experience had opened his eyes, and I didn't doubt him. They were certainly wide open when I saw him being dragged alongside my car. He wanted a fresh start in life, he said, and intended to make a living at the motorway services, possibly as a petrol pump. I wished him well and reminded him that if he seriously wanted to be a petrol pump, it would be advisable for him to give up smoking, or at least cut down.

Three hours later I was trundling up a narrow country lane, heading towards my camping site. I hadn't trundled for years, but somehow, with tall, thick hedges either side of me, poor vision through my insect-covered windscreen, and the thought that any minute now a farmer's van could come hurtling round the bend towards me and cause a horrifying, possibly fatal collision, a trundle seemed appropriate. I'd seen the sign a couple of miles back on the main road.

'Camping Site Ahead. Turn left at Haunted Gallows Hill. Right at Dead Man's Wood. Then sharp right at Rotting Maggoty Decomposed Corpse's Pond.'

It all sounded so delightfully rustic! And there it was,

'Gravestone Acres Camping Site. Hot and Cold Showers. Followed by Some Sunny Periods and the Chance of Snow Flurries Later.'

I pulled up outside the camp office and tooted my horn. The door of the office creaked open and a tall grey-haired man in his fifties, with dark rings under his eyes, slowly wandered towards me, carrying a big red book.

'So this is what Michael Aspel does when he's not on the telly' I thought. This man, however, was much older than Michael, and fatter. In fact, he looked nothing like Aspel. The man leaned through my car window, banging his head on the glass because I hadn't rolled it down.

'Good afternoon,' I said cheerily. He just nodded and handed me the red book.

'I'm the campsite manager. You must sign the book. All visitors must sign the book on arrival,' he said. So I did as he asked and, with a flourish, signed it

'On Arrival'

He pointed the way to the top field. *'That's the way to the top field, you should be safe enough up there tonight,'* he said, turning to go back into the office. What did he mean,

'You should be safe enough?'

I got out of my car and followed him inside. I got straight to the point.

'What did you mean when you said I should be safe enough in the top field?' He looked a bit sheepish. Perhaps it was his thick coat of virgin wool, his habit of chewing grass and his tendency to say

'Baaaa'

every couple of minutes. He walked to the other side of the office and rubbed his chin thoughtfully. Then he rubbed it again carelessly. Then he rubbed it a third time. He was getting quite good at it.

He opened a filing cabinet. 'Will you take a drink with me?' he asked, taking out a mature thirty-year-old Scotch. The thirty-year-old's name was Jamie McTavish, of the Pitlochry McTavishes. Jamie was living, only temporarily of course, in the filing cabinet, rent free, until he could find a suitable piece of office furniture big enough for his family of seven.

'So, tell me about the top field,' I demanded. 'Then tell me about the bottom field. Then tell me why birds fly south in winter and where I can find a quaint old-fashioned ironmongers that has that peculiar yet strangely welcoming odour of paraffin, floor polish and the proprietor's armpits.'

It didn't seem an unreasonable request.

'Are you afraid of the dark?' he asked, taking a swig from a hip flask. Well, the flask might have been hip twenty years ago, with its engraved portraits of Starsky and Hutch, but today it seemed no more than a relic of a distant, wraparound-cardigan age.

'I'm not afraid of the dark. I'm afraid of what might be in the dark,' I said - thinking,

'Blimey, that was clever, Joe!'

'Well, if you spend tonight in a tent on the top field, you'll find out exactly what's in the dark,' he said, before laughing like a drain. I couldn't make out whether it was a good impression or not, because I'd never actually heard a drain laugh before, though I had heard my bathwater gurgle down the plughole many times. But as a fellow professional I thought I should give him the benefit of the doubt and applauded his efforts, even shouting 'More!' and 'Bravo!', before standing on the table and emitting ear-piercing whistles.

'Are we talking ... ghosts?' I ventured.

'We are,' he confirmed.

'Will you tell me who the ghost is?' I enquired.

'I will,' he nodded. He leant forward slowly, then he leant sideways quickly. He followed this with a back-flip, a double somersault and a

breath-taking pirouette. He was obviously a man who felt totally at ease in other people's company. My applause was spontaneous. He graciously accepted the bouquet I presented to him and, after cutting the stems and placing them in a rusted old coal scuttle that doubled as a vase, he continued.

'Two hundred years ago, where these fields are today, this area was ... all fields,' he whispered.

I closed my eyes and tried to picture it, but the images escaped me. I looked out of the window at all the fields around me and yes, I could just about picture the place as it must have looked then. Fields as far as the eye could see, possibly a little bit further than that.

'This farm was owned by a wicked man named Septimus Throttle. His name sent shivers down the backs of all who knew him and shivers down the fronts of all who didn't know him! He was cruel and heartless and treated people like animals. You've heard of a bad egg? Septimus Throttle was a six-egg omelette! He was also a penny-pincher. Penny was the barmaid at the local inn, a rough sort of establishment by all accounts, called 'The Tattooed Arms'. He'd set his cap at her, but she didn't look good in a cap, preferring a more maidenly bonnet. He asked her to marry him on many occasions. Why he wasn't content to marry her just the once, I don't

know, but she refused because she was in love with a young blacksmith named Harry Guard. Or was he a young blackguard named Harry Smith? No matter.

'Penny and Harry used to do their courting on the top field and when Septimus found out that Penny was in love with Harry, he hired two local villains, Bob Identical and Ted Identical, the Identical twins, to do young Harry in. One night, while he was waiting to meet his sweetheart, they set upon him with their bagels. They should have used cudgels, but this was to be quite an orthodox murder.

Just before he died, however, Harry, who was a blacksmith by trade, took out his metal hammer and four horseshoes and, with his last breath, lunged at his assailants and shod them both through the heart!

'Moments later, Penny arrived to keep her date with Harry, only to find him and the Identical twins sprawled on the ground ... dead. The sight of the love of her life lying there was too much for the delicate girl and her little heart stopped beating.

'Later that day, Septimus Throttle came looking for the two murderers, to hand them their *fee for doing the dastardly deed, and when he saw all four bodies he turned his horse round to race back to his house. But on the way, his horse tripped on a discarded gobstopper and he fell off his mount, breaking his worthless neck. Thus, in one afternoon, the top field was strewn with five bodies!'*

The campsite manager stopped talking, struck a match and set light to his pipe. It burst into flames and he deftly threw it in the bin. I hadn't seen anything quite so deft for some time. He stared at the floor. The only sound was the clock on the wall, relentlessly ticktocking, ticktocking the seconds away, and the rustle of flames as a pile of newspapers he'd thrown in the bin earlier became a fierce but containable blaze.

As I poured coal scuttles full of water into the bin in an attempt to put out the mini-inferno, the manager ignored me and just looked down at his feet. He was in no position to stare UP at them.

Eventually I thought it best to say something. I had to. Numerous hours had passed and I was getting hungry.

'So, is it all right for me to pitch

my tent in the top field?' I asked.

'So you don't believe my story then?' he said.

'I'm sure that incident happened in the top field all those years ago, but I don't think all five of them still wander around up there, night after night, moaning and groaning and clanking chains. It would be too horrible to contemplate. Like a never-ending Nolans' concert!'

'That's as maybe,' he said. *'But I'm off home now and I won't be back until seven o'clock tomorrow morning. So you're on your own'.*

'But what about all the other campers?'

'There aren't any. This is the last week of the season. Once you pitch your tent up there, you'll be the only soul for miles around.' He shivered. *'The only living soul, anyhow!'*

Then he put on his overcoat, climbed into his battered old Cortina and drove off down the mud-encrusted path.

So, at around 4.30 p.m., with the afternoon sun fading rapidly, I strolled up the hill to the top field and began to pitch my tent under the protective branches of the Drowned Witches' Oak. Bearing in mind that this was my first attempt at putting up a tent, I was more than pleased to have completed the job just six and a half hours later. The tent wasn't completely erect. Well, it wasn't erect at all to be honest. I just stuck the tent pole in the ground, leaned up against it and wrapped the tent around me like a blanket. I went over all the things that had happened to me that day. Finding the lost camping shop ... the bit of luck in finding a newsagent with a tent for sale ... his wife regaining consciousness after all those years ... his complete indifference to the incident ... then the poor devil being dragged alongside my car for miles ... meeting the old campsite manager, whose name I still didn't know ... and his tall tale about the murder on the very site where I was camped. I closed my eyes and drifted off into a deep sleep. I woke to the sound of twiglets snapping. I'd bought a small family-size packet at the motorway services and had forgotten that I'd put them in my back pocket. By turning over in my sleep I'd broken them into a large family-size packet. Then I heard it. It wasn't quite a moan, it wasn't quite a groan and it was coming closer. It was pitch dark and I can remember wishing the pitch had been floodlit. My teeth started chattering, but I made them stop. This was no time to gossip.

I peered into the darkness. I peered for ages. It was the longest peer in history. Blackpool would have been jealous. Still that strange sound came closer and closer. I looked at my watch in the pale moonlight. It was just past

1.00 a.m. next Thursday week!! I decided that I must think about buying a watch instead of winning another one in an amusement arcade!!!

Suddenly I saw it. A tall, ghostly shape coming up the hill from the direction of the camp office. It had its arms out in front, and from its mouth came this horrible rasping sound. Closer it came, ever closer, and I sank deeper and deeper into the folds of my tent, hoping it wouldn't see me.

'Get back,' I shouted. 'Get back, oh get back to where you belong.'

It stood over me, still making that rasping noise, rather like the sound a broken accordion might make. Even in the moonlight I couldn't make out who, or what, it was.

'Who, or what, are you, oh spirit? Harry Smith? Septimus Throttle? Or one of the Identical twins?' I asked, nervously.

It got down on the ground next to me and tapped me on the arm. With a hoarse whisper it spoke.

'It's me, Ron, the campsite manager. We met earlier. Blimey, my chest is playing me up something rotten tonight. I sound like a broken accordion!'

He took a deep breath.

'Walking up that hill fairly creased me.'

'What are you doing up here?' I asked. I looked at my watch again. 'Nine o'clock on the evening of Whit Monday, 1985?'

'There was something important I forgot to ask you,' he said.

'Couldn't it wait until the morning?' I asked. 'You almost gave me a little bit of a fright. Very nearly.'

'No. If you're camping on this land, there's something you should know!'

'About the murders and the ghosts?'

'Yes, you told me!'

'No, not all that nonsense. The reason I drove back here at this time of night was to ask this ...' He took a medicinal swig from his Starsky and Hutch totally un-hip flask.

'Do you ... do you know the Country Code?'

'Of course I do!' I exclaimed. 'Now can you leave me in peace?'

'Do you know the part about stinging nettles and what you're not supposed to do near them?'

'Yes, I know that bit too!' I just wanted him to go. After all it was 3.05 p.m ... July 35th 1772, according to my watch.

'Right, I'll leave you in peace then,' he said, getting up and taking a deep, therapeutic breath. *'Ahhh! That's better.'*

He looked at my pathetic attempt at putting up a tent, but he didn't pass any comment. He wasn't able to, being doubled up with hysterical laughter.

Eventually, having calmed down, he asked

'Have you eaten?'

'Err, no. I can't sleep on a full stomach.'

'Are you hungry?' he asked.

'Not really. Why do you ask?'

'Well, about three miles up the main road there's a transport café that serves the best bacon, eggs, tomatoes and fried bread in the county. I might stop off there on the way home.'

I pretended not to be interested, but the saliva dripping from my mouth gave the game away.

'It's open twenty-four hours. Come on, it's my treat. I must have put the wind up you something terrible tonight, lad.'

We laughed as we made our way down the hill to his car. We got in and as soon as he put the heater on and we were driving down the lane, I forgot all about ghosts and legends. All I could think about was a plate of hot food.

'By the way, I'm Joe. Joe Pasquale,' I said. 'And you're Ron, aren't you?'

He kept his eyes on the road ahead as he said, in a strange, half-amused voice, *'Yes, Ron's the name I'm known as around here, but that's not my real name!'*

I suddenly felt a chill, despite the warmth of the car. I tried to stop myself, but I had to know. I had to ask:

'Oh, so what's your real name, then, Ron?'

He turned to look me straight in the eye as he said slowly:

'Haven't you guessed yet, Joe? It's Septimus Throttle!'

Trying to sound brave as I attempted to open the car door and leap out, I ventured

'It's not really, is it?'

He turned his gaze back to the road again and laughed like a drain. This time it sounded pretty much like gurgling bathwater.

'No. I'm only pulling your leg. Sorry, mate! No, I'm just Ron the campsite manager and I think I owe you an extra round of toast for that last prank. You should have seen your face!'

We laughed ourselves silly all the way to the transport café, but we stopped laughing when we got there. It was open twenty-four hours a day, but today wasn't the day.

So that was my last camping holiday, and when I say my last I mean my last. I know there are thousands of you who love the outdoor life and think roughing it is great fun, but it's not my idea of relaxing. Let's put it this way. The only time I'll ever sleep under canvas again is if I hang a Rembrandt over my bed.

So if you are thinking of a camping holiday, don't forget to follow the Country Code, because if you forget to close a gate after you the sheep won't half feel the draught.

If you ever find yourself at the **Gravestone Acres Camping Site** and you pitch your tent in the top field, here's a friendly word of warning. When it gets dark and the north wind is whistling through the gnarled branches of the **Drowned Witches' Oak** and you get a strange, unsettling feeling that chills you to the bone, whatever you do, don't do it too close to the stinging nettles!

nutty nurs

Little Miss Muffet sat on her tuffet,
But it didn't do any lasting damage.

Old Mother Hubbard
Went to the cupboard,
And the salesman said
'We can deliver it today
if you're interested, Madam!'

Incey-wincey spider, climbing up the spout,
I'm not ordering a pot of tea in that cafe again!

Simple Simon met a pieman going to the fair,
Said Simple Simon, 'You're wasting your time!
The fair ended two days ago. And they call ME simple!'

There was a crooked man,
But a couple of weeks of physiotherapy sorted him out.

Little Bo Peep has lost her sheep
And doesn't know where to find them.
Well if SHE doesn't know, how the hell can WE help?.

Georgie Porgie, Pudding and Pie,
Failed his cholesterol test, naturally!

*M*ary, Mary, quite contrary.
Who cares HOW your garden grows, you miserable cow.

*T*he Grand Old Duke Of York,
He had 10,000 men,
He marched them up to the top of the hill,
Then he marched them down again.
That guy needed to get himself a hobby!

ery rhymes

*B*aa baa black sheep, have you any wool?
'What's this on my back, you idiot, NYLON?'

*L*ittle Jack Horner sat in a corner,
Stuck-up little sod!

*J*ack and Jill went up the hill
To fetch a pail of water,
Jack fell down and broke his crown,
So Jill had to carry the full pail of water
down the hill all by herself. Men!!

*M*ary had a little lamb,
But she refused the new potatoes.

Seven Days In The Life of Joe Pasquale

(EXTRACTS FROM HIS PERSONAL DIARY)

MONDAY

8.00 a.m. I cooked myself an enormous breakfast. Bacon, eggs, tomatoes, sausage, fried bread and mushrooms. Washed down with three mugs of tea. Brilliant!

8.30 a.m. Got out of bed.

8.31 a.m. Jumped into the shower.

8.55 a.m. Jumped into the car.

9.03 a.m. Jumped a red light.

9.08 a.m. I'm feeling decidedly jumpy today.

10.00 a.m. Had a dental appointment, so decided the dentist would be the best person to see about it.

10.15 a.m. The dentist told me I should have a filling, so I asked him for egg mayonnaise with a sprinkle of black pepper.

10.40 a.m. His receptionist made me an appointment for six months. That seems a long time to spend at the dentists. I might ask him if I can go home for Christmas.

11.30 a.m. Went to the watch menders and told him my watch had stopped. He said it was supposed to. It was a stop watch. He didn't like me calling him 'Mr Watchmender'. He said his proper title was 'a horologist', so I asked him what the future had in store for Capricorns.

My watch needed mending because it was gaining every day. In fact it was gaining so many hours a week, unless it was fixed, by the end of the year I'd be 158.

I asked to look at some new watches and he asked me if I'd given any thought to something with a Swiss movement. I told him that as a matter of fact, I'd given Swiss movement a lot of thought and I'd decided that those men who dance around in leather shorts and slap their knees to accordion music are very silly indeed.

He put a selection of watches on the counter for me to choose from, but it was impossible for me to pick one out. I'd left the shop ten minutes before.

WEDNESDAY

3.45 p.m. I keep thinking it's Tuesday.

TUESDAY

3.46 p.m. It is Tuesday!

THURSDAY

7.00 p.m. Settle down in front of the TV.

9.30 p.m. Switch on the TV.

FRIDAY

5.00 p.m.
The weekend starts
here! Whoopee! Look
out world - here
I come!!

7.30 p.m.
Have an early
night with a cup
of milky cocoa.

SATURDAY

2.00 p.m. Drove
to my local
multiplex cinema.
I wanted to
drive to the dry
cleaners, but there's
something wrong with the steering.

2.15 p.m. There are eighteen different films on here.
I get a headache trying to watch them all.

2.25 p.m. A crowd of people down the front were shouting
and swearing and getting very violent. I called the manager
to complain, but he said that that's what actors do in films
these days.

2.50 p.m. Bought a giant bucket of popcorn. Started
eating it.

5.30 p.m. Almost half-way through the popcorn.

10.40 p.m. Nearly finished.

SUNDAY

8.40 a.m I've never had bacon and popcorn before. Mmmm!

11.00 a.m Go for a walk to the newsagents and buy every Sunday paper on his counter. Put them all under my right arm and walk home.

11.40 a.m. Have to go to Casualty to have my right shoulder put back into place. Must remember to buy only ONE paper next Sunday or take a wheelbarrow.

1.00 p.m. Enjoy a traditional Sunday roast. Chicken, roast potatoes, peas, gravy ... and stacks of popcorn.

2.30 p.m. Decided to get in the car and go for a drive in the country. Looking through the windscreen, I saw wood pigeons, magpies, jackdaws, kingfishers, foxes, hares, rabbits, squirrels, hedgehogs and a cuddly old badger. I still have no idea how they got into my car.

10.30 p.m. Locked up for the night, switched the burglar alarm on, made sure all twenty-seven security lights were working and the electrified fence was up and running. Put the guard dogs out to roam the grounds and fed the piranhas who swim in the moat.

10.45p.m. I don't know HOW they broke through all my high-tech security systems, but they did! It was a nightmare I wouldn't want anyone to endure. I had to spend almost an hour looking at my next-door neighbour's holiday snaps!

Rabbit

shopping List
1. milk
2. bread
3. beans
4. apples
5. ice-cream

MY
GUIDE TO
PROFESSIONAL
SHOW
BUSINESS

I get lots of letters from people wanting to know how to break into this business we call 'show', and I give every letter the same response. None.

Someone once said that stand-up comedy is the hardest job in the world. I think he was watching me when he said it.

In the clubs and pubs, caravan parks and holiday camps, there are hundreds of people daydreaming of becoming professional comics. I just hope they're not operating heavy machinery at the time.

So, for what it's worth **(£1.99 plus VAT)**, here's the true story of how I got into show business. I hope it puts most of you off, because I haven't got a very strong act, so I don't need the competition.

I knew from a very early age that I had a highly developed sense of humour. My first performance was in the delivery room when I was just a couple of minutes old. I went into a routine about how pleased I was to move into a brand new neighbourhood where people took an interest, because where I'd just come from, I'd been totally ignored for nine months!

It didn't go down too well. In fact one lady, wearing a blue uniform, actually held me upside down and slapped my backside. I realised then that I needed some new material.

At my first school I was made to stand in the corner every day, not that I was naughty or anything. It just happened that there was a nasty damp patch in the corner and, as my yellow jumper matched the rest of the paintwork, my teacher thought it would be easier on the eye if I stood in front of it.

I wasn't very good at scrapping and soon learned how powerful comedy could be in defeating the class bully.

Whenever he tried to have a go at me, I belted him with the Bob Monkhouse Bumper Joke Book.

I did quite well at my exams. I only fell asleep during one of them.

My careers master asked me what I'd like to do when I left school. I told him I wanted to have my tea and watch the telly with my dad, like I do every night.

I had no idea what I wanted to do for a living until that magical night I was taken to my first panto. As soon as the lights went down and those gorgeous red velvet curtains parted, I knew exactly what I wanted to do with the rest of my life. It seemed an impossible ambition. How could a kid from my background ever aspire to a career as a red-velvet curtain maker?

The day the circus lorries drove into town, I was entranced by all the glitter, colour and excitement. I'd never seen a lorry before.

The clowns were the ones that I identified with. Those baggy clothes ... those big made-up eyes

and red lips ... that orange hair. They all looked like my nan!

Then one day I was walking outside the London Palladium when I looked up at the big neon display that said 'London Palladium' and the hairs on the back of my neck stood up. I thought 'This is a sign!'

The final test happened the exact same day, as I walked across Shaftesbury Avenue and got knocked down by a car driven by Bernard Delfont. It was nothing serious, just some paintwork off the front of his Rolls Royce where his bumper was imbedded in my leg, and I thought 'Yes. It's official. I've got show business in my blood!'

I did the rounds of all the London agents. When they weren't interested I did the rounds of all the Manchester, Birmingham, Liverpool and Bristol agents. When they weren't interested, I did the rounds of every agent in every city, town, village and hamlet until, at last, I found an agent in a small northern town who was

willing to risk his own money on my future. He gave me my train fare home and told me to stop wasting everyone's time.

I was devastated. I'd have to do what I had promised my parents, and settle down in a proper job. But fate was waiting in the wings. One of the agents I'd seen in London urgently needed someone young, funny and good looking and, as it was an emergency, picked me. I was to report to Topps Holiday Village first thing the next morning. I was going to be one of the famous Topp Coats!

Naturally, on my first day there I came down to earth with a bang. Some little oik pushed me out of my monorail car.

I learned a lot at Topps. For the first couple of weeks, as a newcomer, I was an 'Under' Topp Coat. Then, after a month or so I was promoted to an 'Over' Topp Coat. I much preferred that to the other vacancy available, which was emptying the litter bins all day. That was the job of the 'Waste' Coat.

My confidence grew.

I learned how to sing, dance, juggle, tell jokes, eat fire, train a sea lion to catch a beach ball, walk a tightrope and play the piano. Then the Entertainment Officer took me to one side and suggested it might be best if I did each of them separately.

On the last night of the summer season, I think it was December 12th, a coach load of agents came all the way from London to see the Topp Coats perform.

I did my act. Two minutes of jokes, two minutes of song and two minutes of magic. I took my bow and walked off to complete silence. I sat in my dressing room and stared at the whisky bottle on the table. I was tempted to open it, but there was nowhere I could spend 900 pennies at that time of night. There was a tap on the door. There was another one in the sink as well.

A man walked into the room, an expensive camel-haired coat slung over his shoulders. It was mine. It had fallen off the back of the door. He looked very distinguished, with grey hair swept back at the temples, a Savile Row suit and cigar. He looked half Italian to me. I would have guessed his name was Gino or Mario and I'd have placed him around fifty-five. Probably an agent or impresario.

'Hello Joe boy!' he said. *'My name's Gino, but my friends all call me Mario. I'm half Italian and I'll be fifty-five next month. I'm an agent, and also a bit of an impresario!'*

I just nodded as if I'd expected him to say that.

'I think me and you can do business,' he said, as he drew up a chair. I took my pen out and drew a bottle of vodka and a couple of glasses and we settled down to a caricature of drinking.

'Joe boy, I think I can make you a star,' he said. *'It'll take time and money and effort, and more money and dedication and lots more money but I think you can do it. What do you say?'* He stubbed out his cigar on the table. I didn't mind. He'd caught three cockroaches who were scrabbling home after watching the midnight cabaret.

'I don't know what to say,' I said.

He told me to come and see him in London the following week and I kept my appointment. Since my days at Topps Holiday Village, it's true to say I've never looked back. In fact I **can't** look back, because of the neck injury I received when that little oik pushed me out of the monorail car.

If you're serious about a career in show business you have to prepare yourself for plenty of heartache, tears, pain and crushing disappointment, and that's just when you watch my act!

If you make it, and some of you will, and you're the number one star of the number one show in town, and one night after a performance you hear a knock on your dressing room door and see me there, a little bit older ... a little bit thinner on top... take a long look at me and let these very important words seep back into your consciousness.

'Write Joe a cheque for £1.99 plus VAT and take him to dinner!'

A CLUMSY TART AND OTHER FAVOURITES

She broke off our engagement,
She really broke my heart,
Then she broke our video,
What a clumsy tart.

Go for a 20-mile walk every day,
Get yourself fit the healthy way.
Then at the end of seven days
You'll be in Walton-On-The-Naze.

Pity the poor armadillo,
It's scaly and ugly and sad,
And the fact there's
no other word that
rhymes with
armadillo
Is making me
ever so mad.

I used to play bingo
each night without
fail,
But I'll never be
going again.
I would have won
SIX full houses
last night,
If I'd only
remembered
my pen!

An extremely posh man called Cyril
Had the bad luck to sit on a squirrel.
The squirrel ran off,
Having startled the toff,
And set up a new home in The Wirral.

I'm not afraid of ghosties,
And I'm not afraid of ghouls.
The only thing I'm scared of
Is I'll never win the pools!

I once spent a weekend in Brighton,
I can't quite remember what year.
All I really recall
Is I had SUCH a ball
And I fell off the end of the pier!!

A delightful young lady
from Sale,
Has skin that's amazingly
pale.
She's been struck by
lightning,
Now her pallor's quite
frightening,
Oh what an incredible tale!

Chocolate gives you pimples,
Sweeties give you spots,
So eat more fruit and vegetables,
Then you can give me all your
chocolates and sweeties.

Less than HALF PRICE for a luxury shopping bag?

HOW DO WE DO IT?

Through bulk shopping! (Most Friday nights) *'Shoppin' Joe Promotions'* proudly present the SUPER 'MARKET' bag!

For only £4.99

we will send you one of our super 'Market' bags, which will hold any number of items. Useful for days out, holidays abroad, and

... particularly for shopping!

Made of durable 'CRINKLY WHITE PLASTIC', this up to the minute bag has two generous handles and is so roomy! Yet it can be folded so that it fits inside your coat pocket!

Available in <u>four</u> stylish designs: the small; the smaller still; the absolutely tiny; the minuscule

If you order within the next seven days, we'll send to you, along with your super 'Market' bag, absolutely free of charge, a luxury rollerpen*, as used by customers of several high street banks!

ONCE YOU'VE GOT ONE, YOU'LL WONDER HOW YOU EVER MANAGED WITHOUT ONE!

IF YOU ARE NOT SATISFIED WITH YOUR SUPER 'MARKET' BAG, PLEASE RETURN IT TO 'SHOPPIN' JOE' AND WE WON'T SAY ANOTHER WORD ON THE MATTER. THAT'S THE SHOPPIN' JOE PROMISE. CASH AND POSTAL ORDERS SHOULD BE SENT TO 'SHOPPIN' JOE PROMOTIONS' MYDOGGIE, BERKS. (IF YOU DO NOT WISH TO RECEIVE REGULAR JUNK MAIL FROM US - MOVE.)

* Some models may have chain still attached.

SPECIAL POP OUT SECTION

MY POP OUT PAGE!

You couldn't possibly read the whole of this book in one sitting, so why not take this opportunity to **POP OUT!**
POP OUT to the pictures, **POP OUT** to the shops,
POP OUT and clean your car. In fact, **POP OUT** and do anything you like.
Then, when you come back, you can read the rest of the book!

History's Forgotten Heroes Remembered

Eddie 'Eddie' Canute

Eddie 'Eddie' Canute
Younger Cousin of King Canute.

In the last days of the fifth-century, life was harsh. King Canute ruled England with a fist of steel. He'd lost his right hand during a grudge duel with Lionel, the greatest swordsman in England. It was a bit of a mismatch really, 'cos Canute's choice of weapon was a balloon on a stick.

Eddie 'Eddie' Canute, the King's younger cousin, was definitely the black sheep of the Canute dynasty. He wore imitation black-leather chainmail with 'STONEHENGE' (a popular heavy metal band of minstrels at the time) written on the back, and he liked nothing better than going for a midnight ride on his Harley. Harley was the name of his black and white pony.

Eddie ran a seedy amusement arcade in Weymouth. Apart from a little illegal mead-dealing on the side, he always managed to keep his nose clean, though he did sometimes have a bogey on the end of it, like we all do from time to time.

He never bothered much with his richer, more royal relative. Oh, they exchanged presents at Christmas. He'd buy King Canute a pair of socks and King Canute would buy him Essex. But they weren't what you would call close, not that I'm presuming that **your** interpretation of the word 'close' is any different from mine. I'm just saying, Eddie and the King weren't ... well, close. They'd fallen out years before, over some silly little thing - I think her name was Fiona. The King wanted her for his wife, but his wife didn't think it was a good swap. Eddie was in love with Fiona, but she left town and eventually settled down with a dragon slayer from Hunstanton.

So imagine Eddie's surprise one warm July morning while, tightening the nuts on a one-armed bandit, he looked up and saw King Canute standing there. He immediately let go of the one-armed bandit's nuts and warned him that if he found him pickpocketing in the area again, he'd make him a no-armed bandit overnight!

King Canute wasn't on his own. He'd brought half the court with him for a paddle in the sea. He stood there looking every inch the monarch, wearing a suit of burnished armour, glinting in the sun, a golden cloak made from the finest silks of the Orient and boots of the softest Moroccan leather. On his royal head, signifying to all who passed before him that he could not possibly be anyone other than the King of England, was a white knotted handkerchief, held in place by a

'Kiss Me Thou Quick'

hat. He made an impressive sight.

Eddie just gave him a cool look, lit a cigarette and leant back against one of those money-grabbing things you always find at the seaside. What do they call them? Landladies!

'Well, well, well,' he said, *'if it isn't King Canute! Or may I call you "Nute"? The last time we met, you were as drunk as one!'*

'Eddie! It's been too long,' said the King, stepping forward to give Eddie a royal hug. 'You look great. Are you working out these days?'

'At the moment, I'm trying to work out what you're doing here today. Haven't you got important kingly things to do, like executing poor people and torturing drawbridge-to-drawbridge salesmen?'

'Eddie, Eddie. You take too much notice of what they're saying about me in some of the papers. Alright, I chop a few heads off now and then, but only on Mondays. If I've got an execution planned for a Monday morning, it gets me through that terrible "Oh no, it's work tomorrow" Sunday-night feeling.' The king smiled. 'Besides, it keeps the people in line. The taxes always get paid on time!' He winked at Eddie, conspiratorially. That was a word Eddie couldn't spell, so he ignored it.

'Look, I'm a busy subject. Tell me what you're doing here or push off back to London,' snarled Eddie. He was quite good at snarling, but he was still working on surly. Surly would take some time.

'Alright, I'll come to the point,' said the King. 'I hear on the grapevine that you stopped the tide coming in,' he said.

'I want you to tell me how you did it.'

'*I don't know what you're talking about,*' said Eddie, momentarily distracted by the sound of a punter winning three groats from one of his machines. '*That should never have happened,*' he reflected, '*it's a chocolate bar dispenser*'.

'I think you do know,' said the King, 'and unless you tell me now, Crazy Olaf here will loosen your tongue!'

Suddenly, the sky seemed to go dark. A huge shadow fell over Eddie. He shivered. Radio Four's breakfast news had been right. There 𝖜𝖔𝖚𝖑𝖉 be a change in the weather at midday. Then he saw him. Eight foot six of muscle and sinew. Bare-chested, shaven-headed, slack-jawed, a man-monster incarnate.

Crazy Olaf towered over Eddie and glowered at him. Eddie had been towered over before and seemed to remember being glowered at once, but this towering 𝖆𝖓𝖉 glowering at the same time made his knees buckle. Eddie thought he was about to be brained by some sort of round, shiny torture instrument on the end of a stick which Olaf had raised above his head. But instead, Olaf placed it in his mouth and took a bite out of it. It was a toffee apple, and he was a messy eater. Drool dribbled down the side of his mouth, his chin and his arm. There was so much of it that by the time it hit the ground, the royal party were ankle deep in it. Eddie couldn't stand any more. '*Alright! I'll tell you about what happened to me and how I stopped the tide coming in.*'

'I thought you might,' said the King, mockingly. He didn't have a black moustache to twirl, so he twirled the moustache of one of his servants instead. She didn't blink an eyelid.

'*The first day I came to Weymouth, I took my deckchair down on to the beach. It was so peaceful, with the water being so shallow, that I thought to myself "Wouldn't it be nice if it could be like this for ever," and I willed the tide not to come in the next morning. It didn't come in the next morning, or the morning after that. Or since!*'

'Such sorcery could be punished by death or two weeks in Eastbourne,' the King said threateningly, 'but, as you've just shared your necromancy with me, I can hardly punish you without punishing myself! So Eddie, I bid you farewell.' The King clapped his hands and his entourage followed him back on to the royal coach - a 52-seater with air conditioning and free tea and coffee facilities.

On the way home, the King decided to stop off at Brighton, just as the tide was coming in, and, stealing a deckchair from under a sleeping pensioner called Gloria from Yeovil, placed it firmly on the sand and willed the tide not to come in. But the tide did come in, with quite a force. The waves were six feet high and there was a tremendous undertow, followed by ten much smaller toes.

King Canute got out of the deckchair and commanded the tide to go back. His courtiers all egged him on, with cries of 'You can do it, your Majesty!' and 'Can I have your stereo now you won't be needing it?'

The tide became fiercer and the waves became stronger and, well, you

know the rest. King Canute was washed out to sea and was never seen again.

Worse still, Gloria's new sandals were ruined and when she got back to her boarding house, she'd missed tea. All in all, a sad day for a lot of people.

The thing is, King Canute could have saved himself a lot of grief if he hadn't rushed off from Weymouth and had listened to Eddie's full story. What the King should have known is that the water in Weymouth Bay is usually always the same depth - the tide hardly comes in or goes out. Whereas in Brighton ...!

So Eddie 'Eddie' Canute went back to his amusement arcade and never made it into the history books. As he said on GMTV at the time 'Why should I care? I had Essex for Christmas! I can make a fortune flogging the 135 square miles of wrapping paper it came in.'

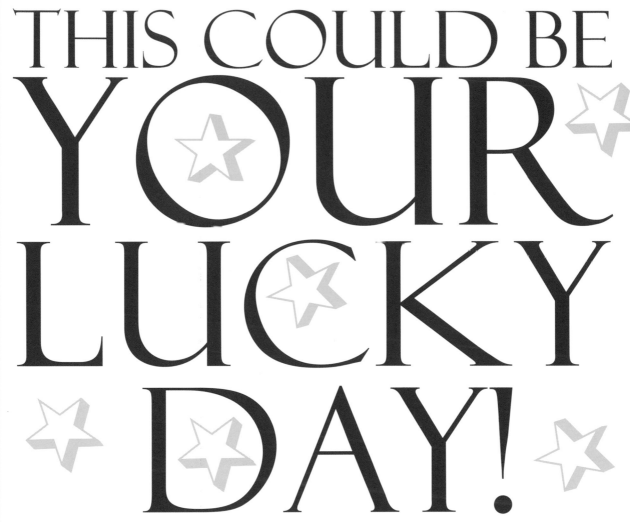

THIS COULD BE YOUR LUCKY DAY!

EVEN IF YOU DON'T READ THIS AD 'TIL TOMORROW

HOW WOULD YOU LIKE TO SAY GOODBYE TO
LIFE'S LITTLE IRRITATIONS?

IT CAN BE DONE.
HOW?
IT COULDN'T BE SIMPLER!

THINGS
ON A
DA

TO DO RAINY DAY

1. Ring up the bank manager and say 'You know that rainy day you told me I should save for? It's today. So I'll be round for my money in an hour!'

2. Start that novel you've always fancied writing. My grandad used to say 'Everyone's got a book inside them,' and in his case it was true. When he was fourteen he swallowed a copy of the world's smallest Bible and he never managed to shift it.

3. Write a long, chatty letter to your old aunt in Shankling - the one you haven't seen for years. While you're at it, write a

long, chatty letter to my old aunt in Shankling who I haven't seen for years.

4. If the rain's getting you down and you need cheering up, get out a couple of old photo albums, because no matter how bad you think you look now, 20 years ago you looked a lot worse. I'm talking 1970s hairstyles ... big ties ... wide lapels! I think you know what I'm getting at! Do you know what the first rule of fashion is? It's this ... Nobody, and I mean nobody, has ever looked good in Union Jack hotpants!

5. Just as the rain starts to come down, say
'Oh no! I was going to mow the lawn, mend the
fence, paint the house, discover Atlantis ...
and now look at the weather!'

6. Change the water in the fish tank, even if they haven't drunk
the last lot you gave them.

7. Ask a duck if he really thinks
it's nice weather.

8. Dust off those ancient old 78s, or
any other elderly relatives who might
be staying with you.

9. Phone Directory Enquiries and ask them what number they require.

10. Turn all the lights out, draw all the curtains and play 'I Spy'. Anyone
who gets one right is either the world's most brilliant guesser or a mole.

11. The rain should have stopped before you get to this one.
If it has, smile and go out and get some fresh air. If it hasn't, you'd
better get the *Yellow Pages* out and look under 'A' for 'Ark builders'.

12. Answer the front door. That'll
be your next door neighbour returning
the lawn mower he borrowed off you the
summer before last.

13. Switch on your new wide-
screen, state-of-the-art, surround-sound,
multi-speaker, cinema-quality, digitally
enhanced colour TV set. There's bound
to be a 1940s black and white film on.

14. Reflect on the highs and lows of your life and remember, you could be a lot
worse off. You could be Jeffrey Archer.

15. Sail a canoe up a creek, throw the paddle away and then see if things
really are as bad as people make out.

16. Play 'Guess how many tea leaves in this tea bag.'

17. Count every tea leaf to see if you're right.

18. Reflect on the irony of the fact that on a day when you're desperate for things to do, it's a total waste of time trying to make another word out of 'rain'.

19. Go outside with a dish of cat food and a dish of dog food and try to find out which of these two species it's raining most.

20. Rummage down the side of the sofa and retrieve everything that's fallen down there over the years. Then have them carbon dated.

21. Take up oil painting. Paper's cheap and oil is only a couple of quid a tin in a car accessory shop.

22. Phone up a double-glazing salesman and tell him you want every window and door in your house replaced, along with every window and door in your holiday home in Majorca and your flat in London. Tell him he has to come around right away or you'll take your business elsewhere. Then hang up.

My Thoughts ... Exactly! Even a madcap, manic, zany, whacky, crazy, side-splitting, off-the-wall, out-of-his-tree, rib-tickling, knee-slapping, elbow-greasing, finger-licking, nose-picking, leg-waxing, stomach-turning, foot-tapping, toe-curling, arm-wrestling, hair-raising, groin-straining, ground-breaking comedy neutron-bomb like me, has a serious side. And, from time to time, I do like to be beside the serious side.

Like many people in this world of comedy we call 'this world of comedy', I rarely talk about my deep fillosoffical ... philla soffikal ... phillowsofickle ... brainy side, that the public never sees. For example, I expect you find it hard to believe that I often lock myself away in my book-lined study for hours, pondering life's many mysteries and conundrums. I sit there, with my eyes closed in concentration, thinking such profound thoughts as 'Where the hell did I put the key to my book-lined study and will I be able to let myself out before "Sooty" starts?'

So, for the first time, here are a selection of my thoughts on a variety of matters. If you're interested in my thoughts on the matter of variety, you'll have to wait for my book on showbiz to appear in the shops. It could be quite a wait - I haven't written it yet.

My Words of Wisdom

(Not to be confused with NORMAN's words of Wisdom which are usually 'Ere, Mr Grimsdale! Why can't I have a proper milk float, instead of this old horse?')

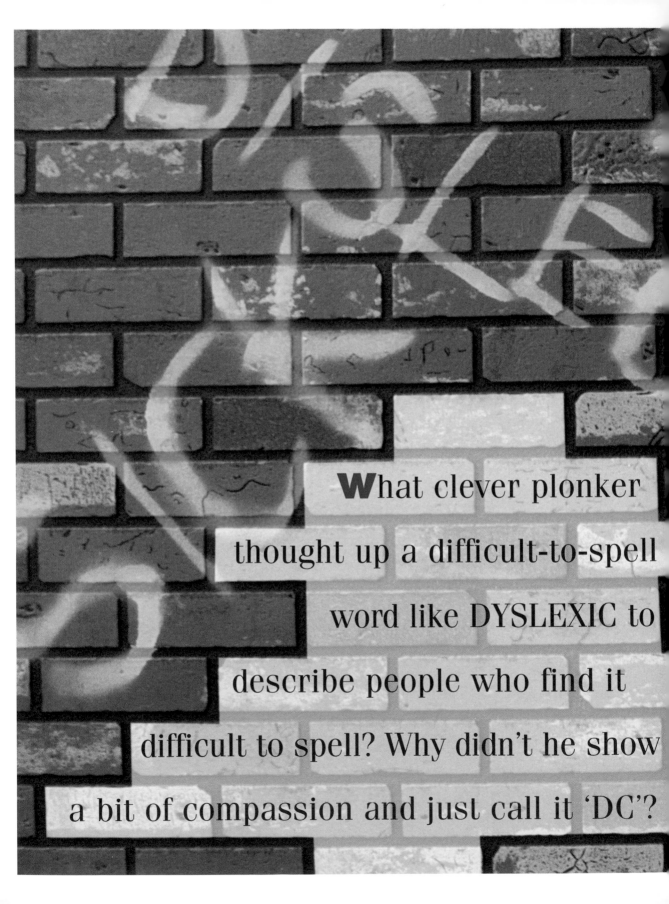

What clever plonker thought up a difficult-to-spell word like DYSLEXIC to describe people who find it difficult to spell? Why didn't he show a bit of compassion and just call it 'DC'?

If prevention really is better than cure, why don't chemists sell us medicine we can take before we get ill?

If someone tells you their dog's bark is worse than its bite, don't believe them. No one has ever gone to the casualty department to have 25 stitches put in their hand because a dog made a loud growling noise at them.

Never look a gift horse in the mouth, especially if you're chewing a lump of sugar at the time.

If a picture paints a thousand words, why did I need to spend all that money on a word processor?

If there are only 26 letters in the alphabet, why is *War and Peace* so long?

A friend in need is a friend indeed. A friend in Marbella, means you'll get a free holiday every year.

If money is the root of all evil, why do churches have collection plates?

When the meek inherit the Earth, who's going to bring the coal in?

It's always good advice to look before you leap, unless you're jumping off the Empire State Building, in which case there's hardly any point.

Never judge a book by its cover. Check out the well-thumbed pages to see if it's worth buying.

If comedy is the new rock 'n' roll, I must be Roger Whittaker.

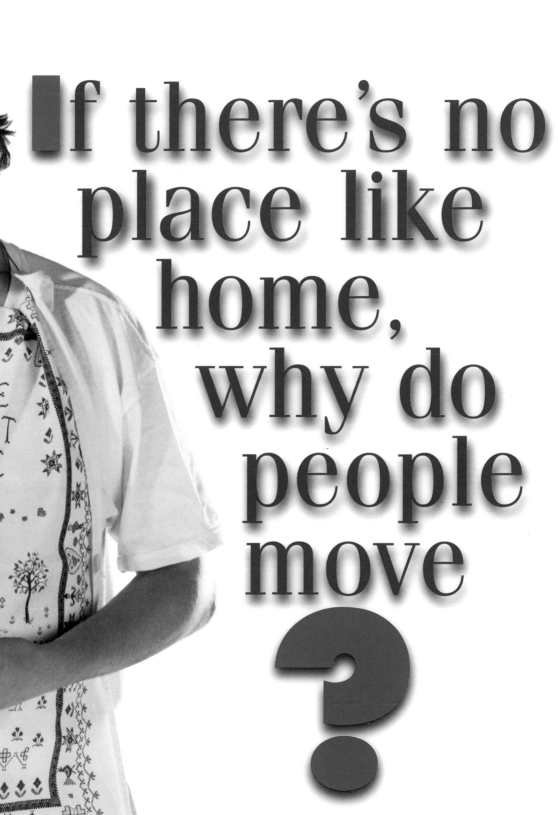

If there's no place like home, why do people move?

Love may be the sweetest thing, but it's fizzy drinks that rot my teeth.

Why do birds suddenly appear, every time you are near? Is it because of all the breadcrumbs in your hair?

If you believe that empty vessels make the most noise, go and sit through a Motorhead concert for a couple of hours and you may change your mind.

If too many cooks spoil the broth, why doesn't someone grab a big ladle and pull a couple out?

Where there's muck there's brass - completely covered in muck.

You are unique in this world. You're a one-off. There is no one else quite like you. And boy, are the rest of us grateful!

Who first discovered that the way to a man's heart is through his stomach? And more importantly, was the operation a success?

Be careful how you treat people when you're on the way up, because the chances are, you'll meet them again when you're on the way down. My uncle told me that. He was a lift attendant.

Don't let that big hit by Wet Wet Wet confuse you. If you really DO feel it in your fingers AND feel it in your toes, it's not love. It's food poisoning!

I don't agree with letting sleeping dogs lie. I've always taught mine to tell the truth, asleep or awake.

If anyone DID try to prove it's easier for a camel to go through the eye of a needle than it is for a rich man to enter Heaven, then what sort of state was the poor camel in when the experiment was over, and was it ever reported to the RSPCA?

Why can't I make another word out of 'ANAGRAM'?

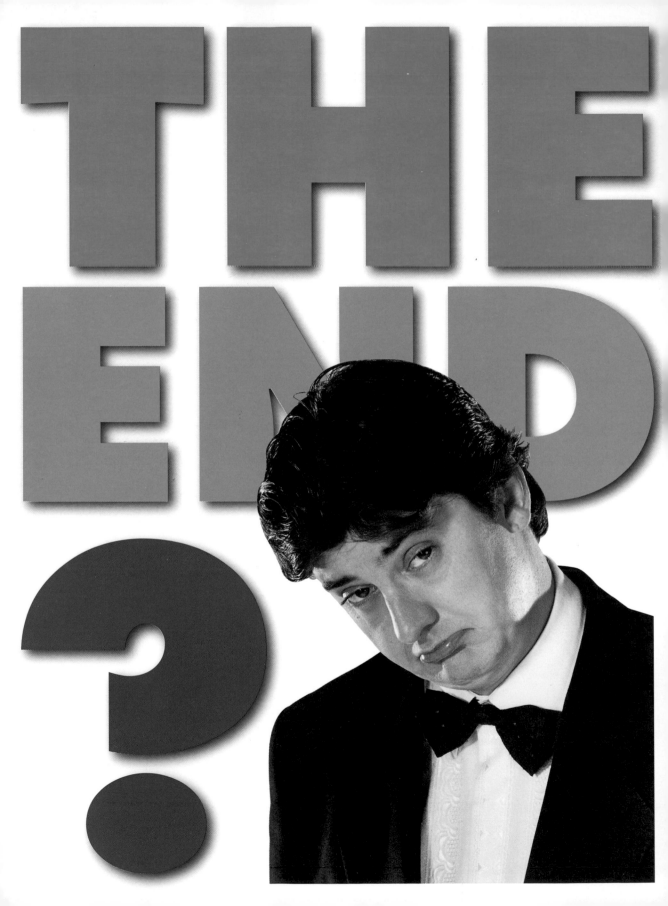